friendly phonics

Fish Can Fly

By Cindy Leaney

Illustrated by Sue King and Peter Wilks

ROURKE CLASSROOM RESOURCES
The path to student success

Note to Parents and Teachers/Educators
Before reading: Ask your child what this book might be about. Read the title aloud together. Then ask what sound *i* makes in *fish* and what sound *y* makes in *fly*. Remind your child to listen for those sounds in the story.

Written by Cindy Leaney
Designed by Ruth Shane
Illustrated by Sue King & Peter Wilks
Project managed by Gemma Cooper

Created and Designed by SGA and Media Management
18 High Street, Hadleigh, Suffolk, IP7 5AP, U.K.

© 2004 Rourke Classroom Resources
P.O. Box 3328, Vero Beach
Florida, 32964, U.S.A.
Editor: Patty Whitehouse

Printed in China

All rights reserved. No part of this book may be reproduced or utilized in any form or by any means, electronic or mechanical, including photocopying, recording, or by any information storage and retrieval system without permission in writing from the publisher.

ISBN 1-58952-902-2

Fish Can Fly

Fish can swim but they can't fly.
Wait a minute—what is that in the sky?

I like kite number five.

I'd like to try and make it fly.

Can I try to fly your kite?

Yes, okay.   Yes, all right.

Let me give you kids a tip.

Hold on tight, don't let it slip.

Pull this side and it will dive.

Pull this one and it will rise.

I wish I could win that prize!

Go ahead. Give it a try.

Make that fish fly way up high!

Look at this kite dip and spin.

I like this! I might win!

Look how well his fish flies!

Kite number five wins first prize!

Game time!

What are the missing letters?

1. h _ _ _

   m _ _ _ t

2. sp _ n

   w _ n

3. s _ ze

   pr _ ze

Answers: **1.** high, might, **2.** spin, win, **3.** size, prize.

How many words can you find in the story that rhyme with *i*?

Answers: fly, sky, high, try.